COUNT GOD'S BLESSINGS
DOT • TO • DOT

EXTREME PUZZLE CHALLENGES, PLUS DEVOTIONS

MARGARET FEINBERG

BETHANYHOUSE
a division of Baker Publishing Group
Minneapolis, Minnesota

© 2018 by Margaret Feinberg, LLC (www.margaretfeinberg.com)

Published by Bethany House Publishers
11400 Hampshire Avenue South
Bloomington, Minnesota 55438
www.bethanyhouse.com

Bethany House Publishers is a division of
Baker Publishing Group, Grand Rapids, Michigan

Printed in the United States of America

ISBN 978-0-7642-3108-7

Scripture quotations marked ESV are from The Holy Bible, English Standard Version® (ESV®), copyright © 2001 by Crossway, a publishing ministry of Good News Publishers. Used by permission. All rights reserved. ESV Text Edition: 2011

Scripture quotations marked GNT are from the Good News Translation—Second Edition. Copyright © 1992 by American Bible Society. Used by permission.

Scripture quotations marked KJV are from the King James Version of the Bible.

Scripture quotations marked NASB are from the New American Standard Bible®, copyright © 1960, 1962, 1963, 1968, 1971, 1972, 1973, 1975, 1977, 1995 by The Lockman Foundation. Used by permission. (www.Lockman.org)

Scripture quotations marked NIV are from the Holy Bible, New International Version®. NIV®. Copyright © 1973, 1978, 1984, 2011 by Biblica, Inc.™ Used by permission of Zondervan. All rights reserved worldwide. www.zondervan.com

Scripture quotations marked NKJV are from the New King James Version®. Copyright © 1982 by Thomas Nelson, Inc. Used by permission. All rights reserved.

Scripture quotations marked NLT are from the Holy Bible, New Living Translation, copyright © 1996, 2004, 2015 by Tyndale House Foundation. Used by permission of Tyndale House Publishers, Inc., Carol Stream, Illinois 60188. All rights reserved.

Author is represented by Christopher Ferebee.

Cover design by Thomas Schwindling

18 19 20 21 22 23 24   7 6 5 4 3 2 1

All the Blessings for You

God gives you more than you can ever imagine. He pours blessing upon blessing on you. Every blessing grounds you in the truth that God is for you, and He extends moments of grace to you each and every day.

He wants to share His goodness, faithfulness, and love with you even more. That's why it's important to take time to pray, journal, and unleash your creative gifts as you reflect on God's promises of blessing.

No matter what situation you're facing, you can find comfort in knowing that God is with you.

God's blessings come in many forms. When you ask for wisdom, He dollops on an extra portion. When you wonder which way to go, He whispers guidance in your heart. When you find yourself at a dead end, He uncovers the path to life.

Your heavenly Father offers a safe sanctuary for hard times. He dispenses peace to those who trust in Him. And He protects you as His beloved child.

No matter how many miles you travel, God promises never to leave or abandon you. He invites you to join Him for all eternity. Scripture reveals that you don't have to question or doubt whether God is with you or for you. He promises, assures, and guarantees His presence and plan for you.

That's why I've created *Count God's Blessings Dot-to-Dot*. Within these pages, you'll find hand-selected verses that reveal God's blessings coupled with ready-to-color dot-to-dot images.

Count God's Blessings Dot-to-Dot invites you to connect the dots in your spiritual life. Consider the following:

- "Those who remain in me, and I in them, will produce much fruit."—John 15:5 NLT
- "I will make up to you for the years that the swarming locust has eaten."—Joel 2:25 NASB
- "They who wait for the Lord shall renew their strength."—Isaiah 40:31 ESV

You'll be awestruck by what you can create with a single line. This is dot-to-dots all grown up—for you. Once you complete the drawing, you can transform the one-dimensional art by adding color and shading to make the artwork pop.

Each of the designs is based on an image or concept from Scripture. There's a devotional reading that will encourage and challenge you. Plus, you'll find space to pray and reflect.

Count God's Blessings Dot-to-Dot provides an opportunity for you to:

- Spend time in prayer and reflection to grow in your relationship with God
- Commit Bible passages to memory to strengthen your faith
- Marinate in the truth of God's blessings and faithfulness
- Discover your creativity as you express your love for God and the Bible
- Strengthen relationships as you invite others to create alongside you
- Share your artistry with others as you display your work

My hope and prayer is that through the upcoming pages, you'll unleash the creative talents God has given you. As you color and draw, you'll whisper the words aloud, commit them to memory, and learn how to walk in greater faith each day.

Blessings,

Margaret

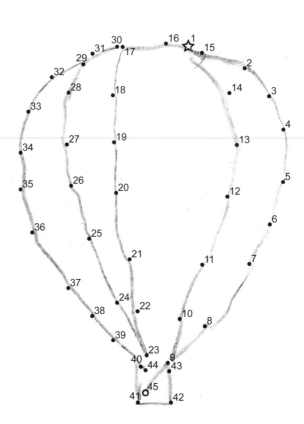

Tips for Extreme Dot-to-Dot

1. Begin by locating the star ☆ to find your starting number one and the open circle ⭕ to locate your finishing mark.

2. Always start with number one. Avoid jumping in halfway or trying to work the puzzle backward.

3. Place your writing instrument on a dot. Then focus your eyes on the next dot where you're heading. Drag your pen until you reach the next dot, which should leave a straight(ish) line. Using relatively straight lines to connect the dots creates the most accurate picture. Practice here.

4. Try not to lift your pencil or pen from the page as you connect the dots. Attempt to complete the drawing in one line.

5. While you can use any writing instrument to complete the drawing, avoid using markers or pens that are too thick. Test your pen on this page before you get started.

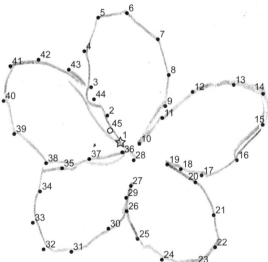

6. You'll find a small finished version of each drawing at the back of this book.

7. Once you've connected the dots, color the page using pens, pencils, or markers.

> See what kind of love the Father has given to us,
> that we should be called children of God; and so we are.
>
> 1 John 3:1 ESV

God calls you His child. That's more than a title or a name. God consecrates you into a forever relationship. God calls you His own. You are an heir and an important part of God's family.

The amount and extent of God's love for you is immeasurable. It's not just the quantity of God's affection, it's also the way God expresses His affection. God's abundant and perfect love is reflected in the person of Jesus Christ, who welcomes us into the fold.

As you reflect on the blessings God has poured over you, allow the truth that you are loved and lovable to seep through your spirit, reaching every part of your being. Though some days you may struggle to see yourself as loved or lovely, the lens of Scripture will broaden your perspective, allowing you to see what God sees.

Take a moment to reflect. How would your attitude, actions, and reactions change if you lived as a beloved child of God? What would it mean to accept that you belong to God's family and are loved unconditionally and immeasurably?

READ • REFLECT • CONNECT • PRAY • JOURNAL

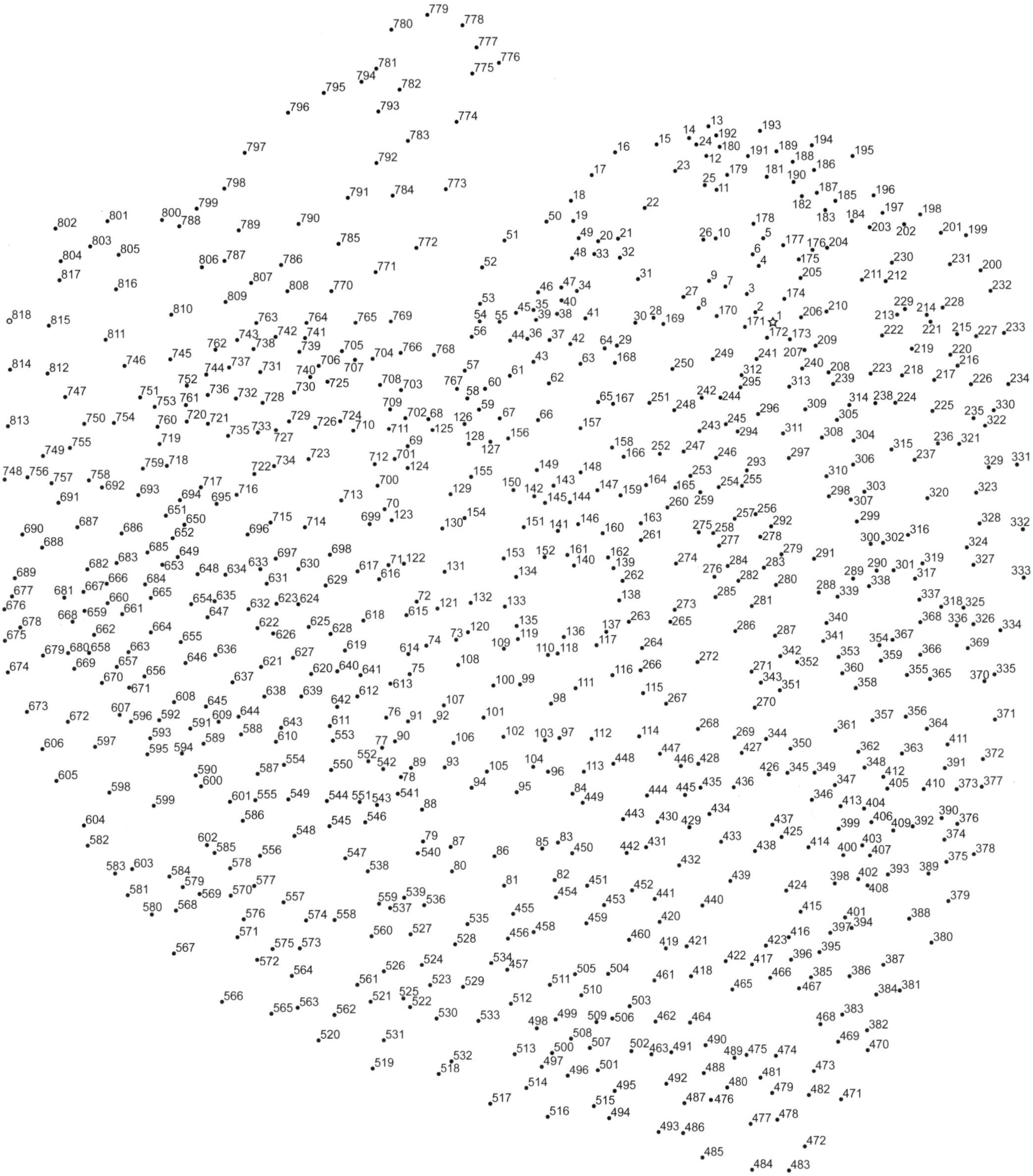

> Some trust in chariots and some in horses,
> but we trust in the name of the Lord our God.
>
> Psalm 20:7 ESV

Horses played a prominent role in ancient times. They were a means of transportation, they symbolized wealth, and they provided an advantage whenever an army entered battle.

Yet the psalmist asks us to remember that the battle is never won by chariots or horses. The battle rests in the hands of God—and we are to trust Him for victory.

This theme of trust appears time and time again throughout Scripture as if God keeps whispering:

What are you placing your trust in?

Who are you placing your trust in?

God emphasizes these questions because they're important: Whatever you place your trust in will become a deity to you.

We tend to trust in what makes people mighty. Thousands of years ago that was chariots and horses. Today, we might look to a school or family or job title or bank account or life plan for security.

In God's fierce love for you, He invites you to turn to Him and trust Him for all things. He is the one who brings the victory.

In what area of your life do you need to trust God right now? What are you currently trusting instead of God? Spend some time in prayer to refocus your trust in Christ.

READ • REFLECT • CONNECT • PRAY • JOURNAL

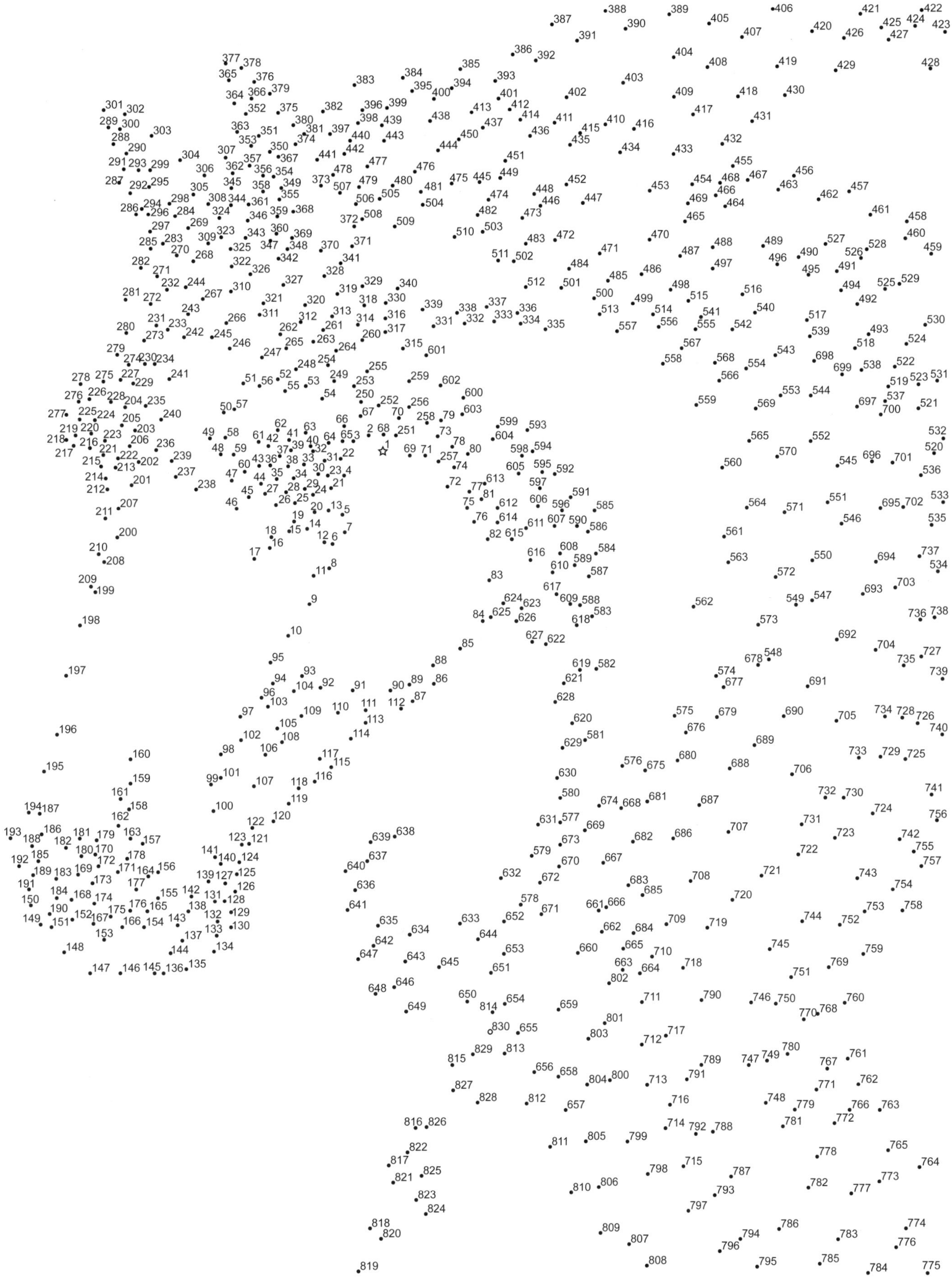

> Come now, let us reason together, says the Lord: though your sins are like scarlet, they shall be as white as snow; though they are red like crimson, they shall become like wool.
>
> Isaiah 1:18 ESV

On January 15, 1885, Wilson Bentley took the first successful photomicrograph of a snowflake. He was only nineteen. This young man from Jericho, Vermont, was touched by the beauty of God found in a snowflake, and he wanted others to see that beauty. At his passing, he left a collection of over five thousand photographs, some of which are still being circulated today. He's the man who discovered that no two snowflakes are alike. Bentley looked at the delicacy of a falling snowflake and couldn't help but reflect on the One who made it.

Scripture equates God's forgiveness to the sparkly white snow. Just as snowflakes blanket the ground during a hushed winter snowfall, covering every dirty sidewalk and street, God's forgiveness covers all, leaving us white as snow. God, who fashioned the delicate features of the snowflake, has the power to transform us, too.

Take a moment to remember that God's forgiveness is available to you right here, right now. Where do you most need to experience God's forgiveness and be washed whiter than snow?

READ • REFLECT • CONNECT • PRAY • JOURNAL

> Then God blessed the seventh day and made it holy, because
> on it he rested from all the work of creating that he had done.
>
> Genesis 2:3 NIV

Since the beginning of time, God has been celebrating *rest* for all of humanity.

Consider the opening story of creation. God places fluorescent fish in their home at the bottom of the sea and hangs stars high in the night sky. Everything swirls as if in awe of what God has done. As a holy explanation point, on the seventh day God doesn't work harder or tweak His design. Instead, God pauses to enjoy the wonder and beauty of all that He has made.

God takes a day off to celebrate His work with rest.

But He doesn't just take the seventh day off to demonstrate what rest looks like; God takes the seventh day off to issue an invitation to us to celebrate our life's work by resting on a regular basis. God invites us to rest so that we, too, are refreshed, rejuvenated, and reawakened to the beauty of His creation.

Where do you need to add a rhythm of rest into your daily and weekly schedule?

READ • REFLECT • CONNECT • PRAY • JOURNAL

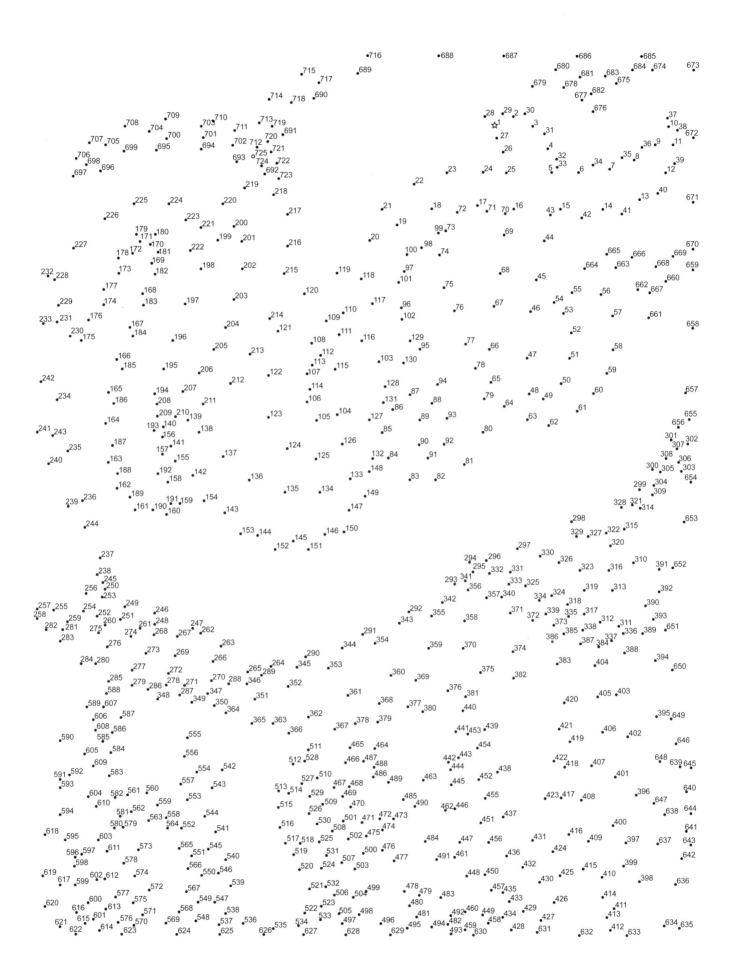

> Then I will make up to you for the years that
> the swarming locust has eaten.
>
> Joel 2:25 NASB

Locusts are a kind of short-horned grasshopper who on their own can be minor irritations, but when they swarm they become serious pests who eat everything in sight. Swarming locusts consume every dot of green forage available: shrubs, woody material, and even paint off buildings.

Scientists note that the average sub-Saharan swarm of desert locusts numbers 50 billion. They can consume four times as much food as all the humans living in New York or London in a single day.

When God promises to make up for the years the swarming locust has eaten, God reveals himself as the ultimate restorer. Though we may look at a situation and think restoration is impossible, God always sees the possibility of making a way where there is no way.

Take a moment to reflect. In what area of your life have you experienced a season of swarming locusts? Ask God to begin a work of restoration and renewal in you so that you can flourish again.

READ • REFLECT • CONNECT • PRAY • JOURNAL

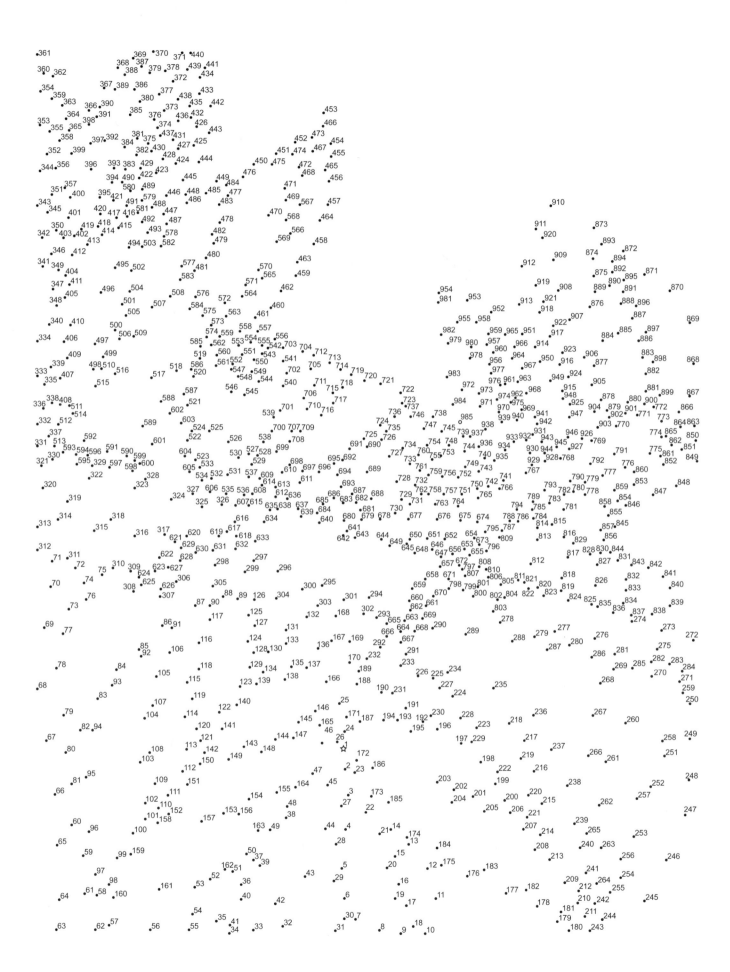

> Yes, I am the vine; you are the branches.
> Those who remain in me, and I in them,
> will produce much fruit.
>
> John 15:5 NLT

Throughout the Gospel of John, Jesus reveals himself through a series of "I Am" statements: the Light of the World; the Way, the Truth, and the Life; the Bread; the Good Shepherd; the Door; the Resurrection and the Life (8:12; 14:6; 6:35; 10:14; 10:9; 11:25). Yet in the final "I Am" saying in the Gospel of John, Jesus boldly declares, "I am the vine" (15:5).

Why does Jesus evoke this imagery to describe himself?

Because vines are a perfect metaphor for what it means to *abide in*. The vine is the source of everything for the branch—every nutrient, every life-giving drop of water, every hint of growth. The branch depends wholly and fully on the vine.

Real fruit bearing is only possible with the life-giving connection to the vine.

Where are you the most fruitful in your life right now? Where do you want to be more connected to the vine who is Jesus Christ? Pause to pray and ask God to produce a more intimate, fruitful relationship with Him.

READ • REFLECT • CONNECT • PRAY • JOURNAL

....

....

....

....

....

....

....

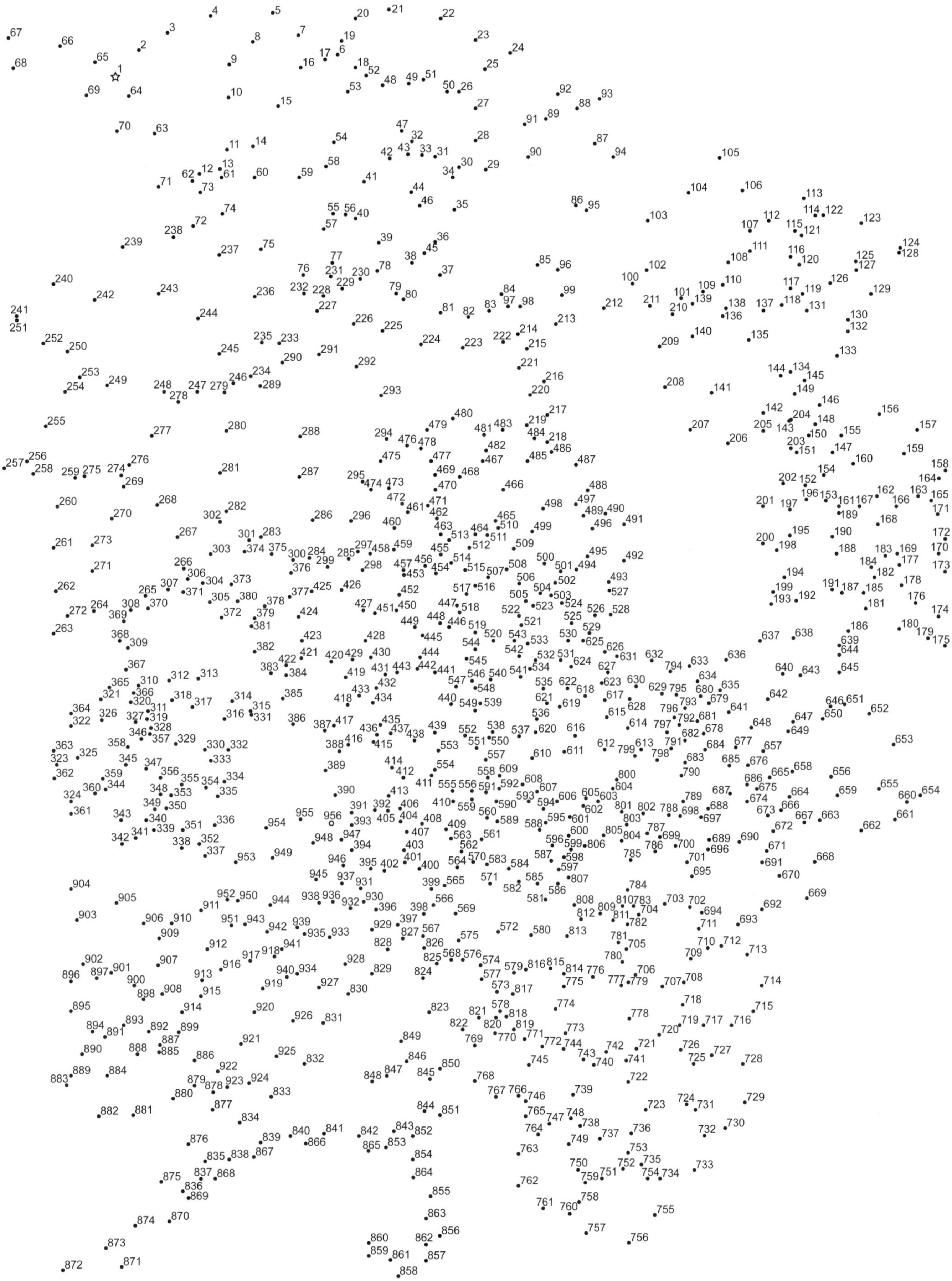

> Which of you fathers, if your son asks for a fish, will give him a snake instead? Or if he asks for an egg, will give him a scorpion? If you then, though you are evil, know how to give good gifts to your children, how much more will your Father in heaven give the Holy Spirit to those who ask him!
>
> Luke 11:11–13 NIV

Sometimes in life it's hard to remember that God is for us. Whenever we experience loss or pain or life doesn't turn out like we expect, we may begin to wonder *God, where are you?* and *God, why have you forgotten me?*

Yet the Bible reminds us that God loves us more than we can fathom and has a hope and a future for us beyond our wildest imaginations.

Jesus teaches us that a good earthly father loves to give good gifts to his children. Jesus says if an earthly father likes to give presents that surprise and delight, imagine how much more your heavenly Father longs to give you.

No matter what you're facing in life, rest assured that God is for you. He promises never to leave you nor forsake you.

What have you given up praying for? Be bold and approach our good and loving Father with the request once more. He welcomes your persistence.

READ • REFLECT • CONNECT • PRAY • JOURNAL

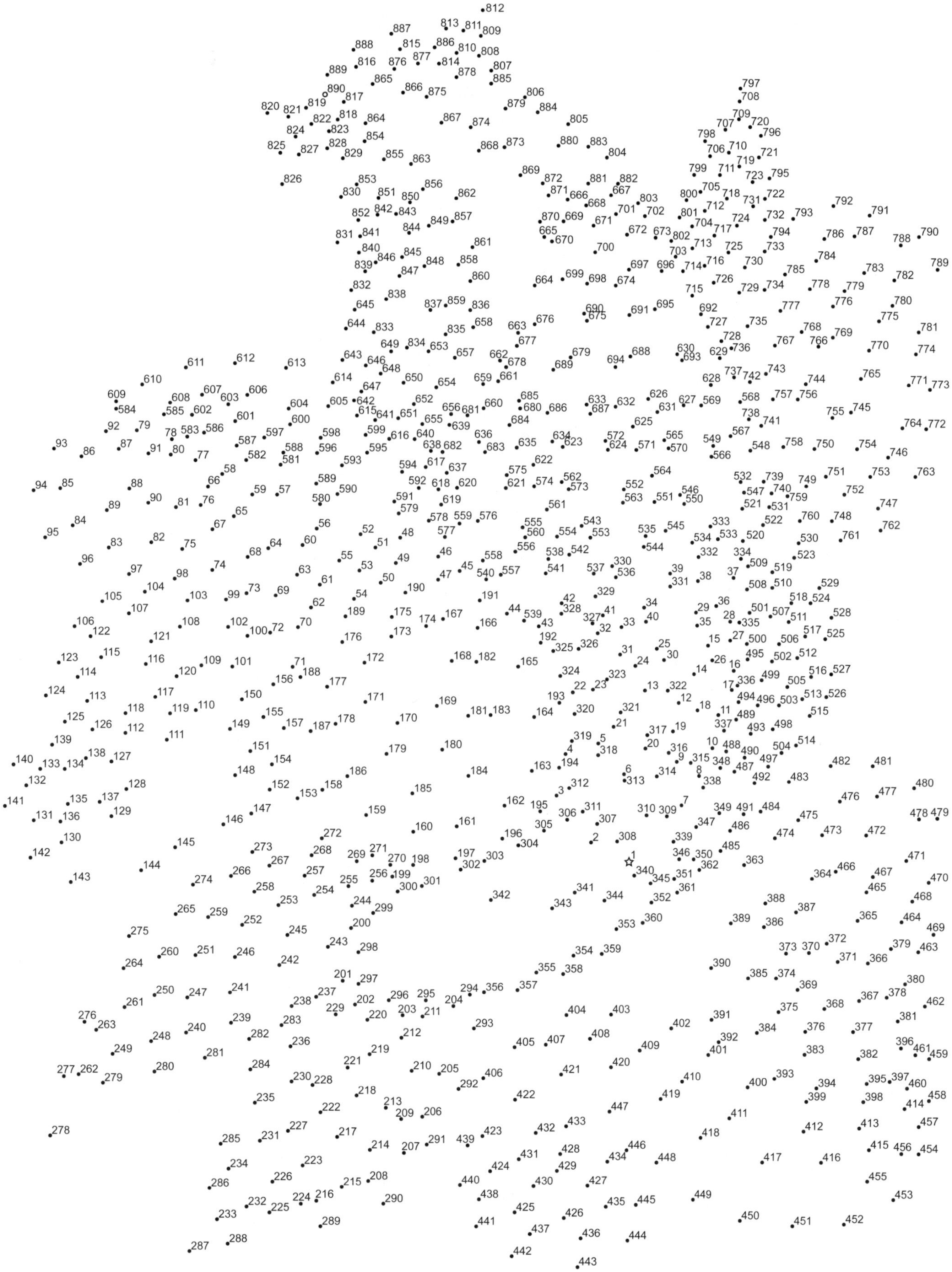

> I have set my rainbow in the clouds,
> and it will be the sign of the covenant
> between me and the earth.
>
> Genesis 9:13 NIV

Did you know that the beauty and wonder of rainbows are created by optics? Light changes directions whenever it passes from one medium to another. This happens because light travels at different speeds based on what it's passing through. When white light passes through a drop of rain during an afternoon shower, the component colors of light slow to different speeds as they enter the droplets. The light and water combine in a way that paints a breathtaking natural work of art.

Following the great flood, God promises Noah that He will never destroy the earth again with water. The rainbow symbolizes God's promise to humanity. The Hebrew word for rainbow, *qesheth*, is the word for an archer's bow. The imagery suggests that God is putting away His archer's bow now that the storm has ended. God uses the optics and imagery of a rainbow to create a work of art in the sky that speaks to both peace and faithfulness.

The next time you see a rainbow—or even a double rainbow—reflect on the goodness of God and His loving commitment to His promises to you.

In what area of your life do you most need to experience God's peace and faithfulness right now?

READ • REFLECT • CONNECT • PRAY • JOURNAL

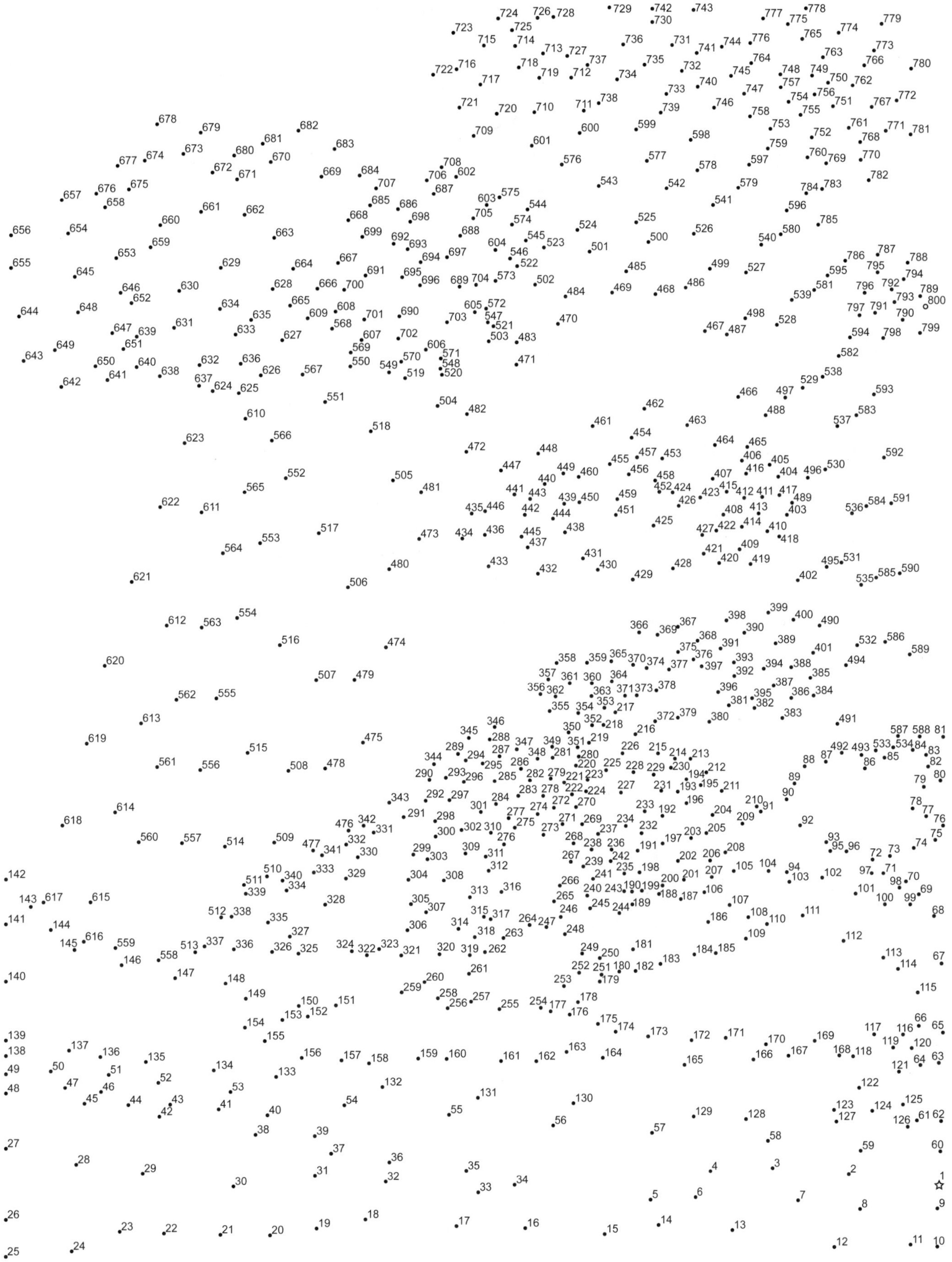

> You will make known to me the path of life;
> In Your presence is fullness of joy;
> In Your right hand there are pleasures forever.
>
> Psalm 16:11 NASB

Sometimes we may be tempted to think of God as reserved or stiff, yet the Bible reminds us that our God is a joyful God. The character of God is brimming with affection, delight, and generosity. God is not just the essence of joy, He's the giver of it, too.

God is so wildly generous with His joy that He doesn't keep it all to himself. He desires to share it with us. God wants His joy to become our joy. There is no greater demonstration of the joy God wants to share with us than is found in Jesus Christ.

The psalmist reminds us that when we pursue the path of life that God makes known to us, we discover joy in the presence of God, who walks with us. And when we find our joy in God, we bring Him glory. That's a fancy-pants, theological way of saying that every day you joyfully walk with God, you put a smile on your heavenly Papa's face.

Write down five things that bring you joy today. How can you spread joy to those around you?

READ • REFLECT • CONNECT • PRAY • JOURNAL

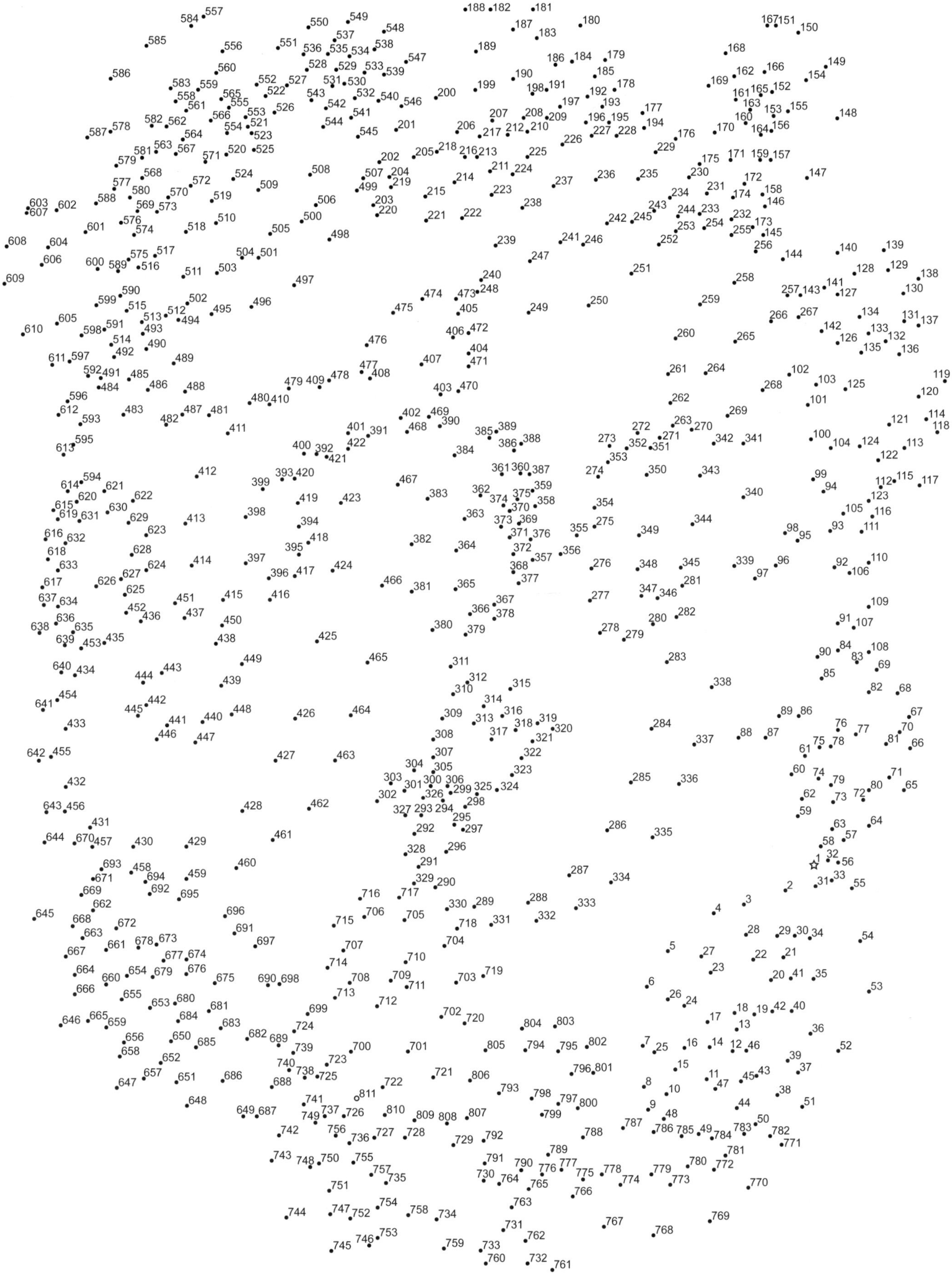

> He makes me as surefooted as a deer,
> able to tread upon the heights.
>
> Habakkuk 3:19 NLT

Did you know there are more than forty different species of deer? In fact, caribou, elk, and moose are considered part of the deer species. They range from tiny—only twenty pounds—to huge—almost two thousand pounds. These social creatures travel in herds. They only eat vegetation, so they scour the landscape, including the mountaintops, for food.

When Habakkuk draws on the imagery of the deer walking on the heights of mountains, he speaks to the strength God gives us and the places God leads us. Deer have a bounding gracefulness. They spring with ease, bounce with lightness. The passage describes the deer bounding on the crest of a mountain. This speaks to the higher places God brings us. He lifts us and draws us closer to himself.

If you find yourself plodding through the low valleys of life, remember that God is the one who will make you as surefooted as a deer so that you may remember from whom you receive your confidence and direction.

Spend time in prayer asking Him to take you to those high places. Thank God for being your constant guide and traveling companion.

READ • REFLECT • CONNECT • PRAY • JOURNAL

> In the future there is laid up for me the crown of
> righteousness, which the Lord, the righteous Judge,
> will award to me on that day; and not only to me,
> but also to all who have loved His appearing.
>
> 2 Timothy 4:8 NASB

In the ancient Greek sporting games, a wreath of garland or leaves was placed on the head of the winner of each contest. This placement symbolized the bestowing of a crown for their victory.

The Bible mentions five crowns followers of Jesus can receive in heaven: the crown of rejoicing (1 Thessalonians 2:19), the crown of glory (1 Peter 5:4), the imperishable crown (1 Corinthians 9:24–25), the crown of life (Revelation 2:10), and the crown of righteousness (2 Timothy 4:8).

The crown of righteousness is promised to all who love Jesus and look forward with great expectation to His return. This is a rich promise and hopeful encouragement. No matter what you're facing—the hardship, the challenge, the difficulty, the pain—rest assured that your reward is Christ for eternity.

Pop over and read the Scriptures that describe each crown. Which of the crowns do you most look forward to receiving?

READ • REFLECT • CONNECT • PRAY • JOURNAL

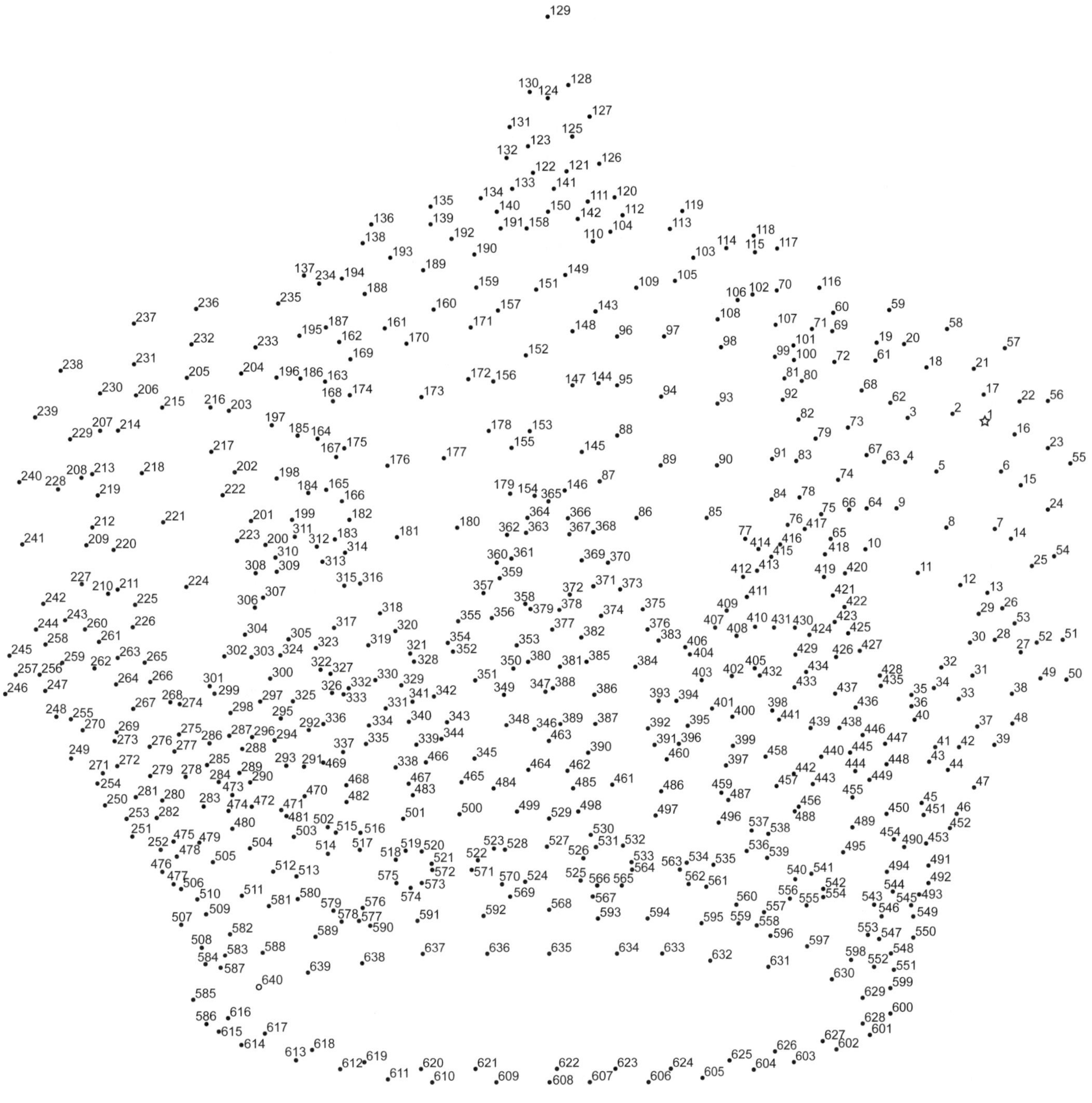

> For all the animals of the forest are mine,
> and I own the cattle on a thousand hills.
>
> Psalm 50:10 NLT

Throughout the psalms, we are reminded that everything belongs to the Lord—the animals, the earth, and all who live in it. This truth is far too easy to forget. God calls us to recognize that what we have isn't really ours. It's all God's.

Why is this so important? First, knowing that all things belong to God means we ought to receive everything we have with a sense of gratitude and humility. Rather than being *possessed* by our possessions, remembering that all things belong to God heightens our responsibility as good stewards.

Second, knowing that God possesses all things sets us free to be more generous. As children of God, we're called and created to share what we have. When we act with generosity, we reflect the generosity that God has already shown us. All good things come from God. When we share what we have with others, we're sharing the goodness of God.

Take a moment to reflect. In what area of your life are you most tempted to be possessed by your possessions? In what areas of your life are you being challenged to give more freely because God has given to you?

READ • REFLECT • CONNECT • PRAY • JOURNAL

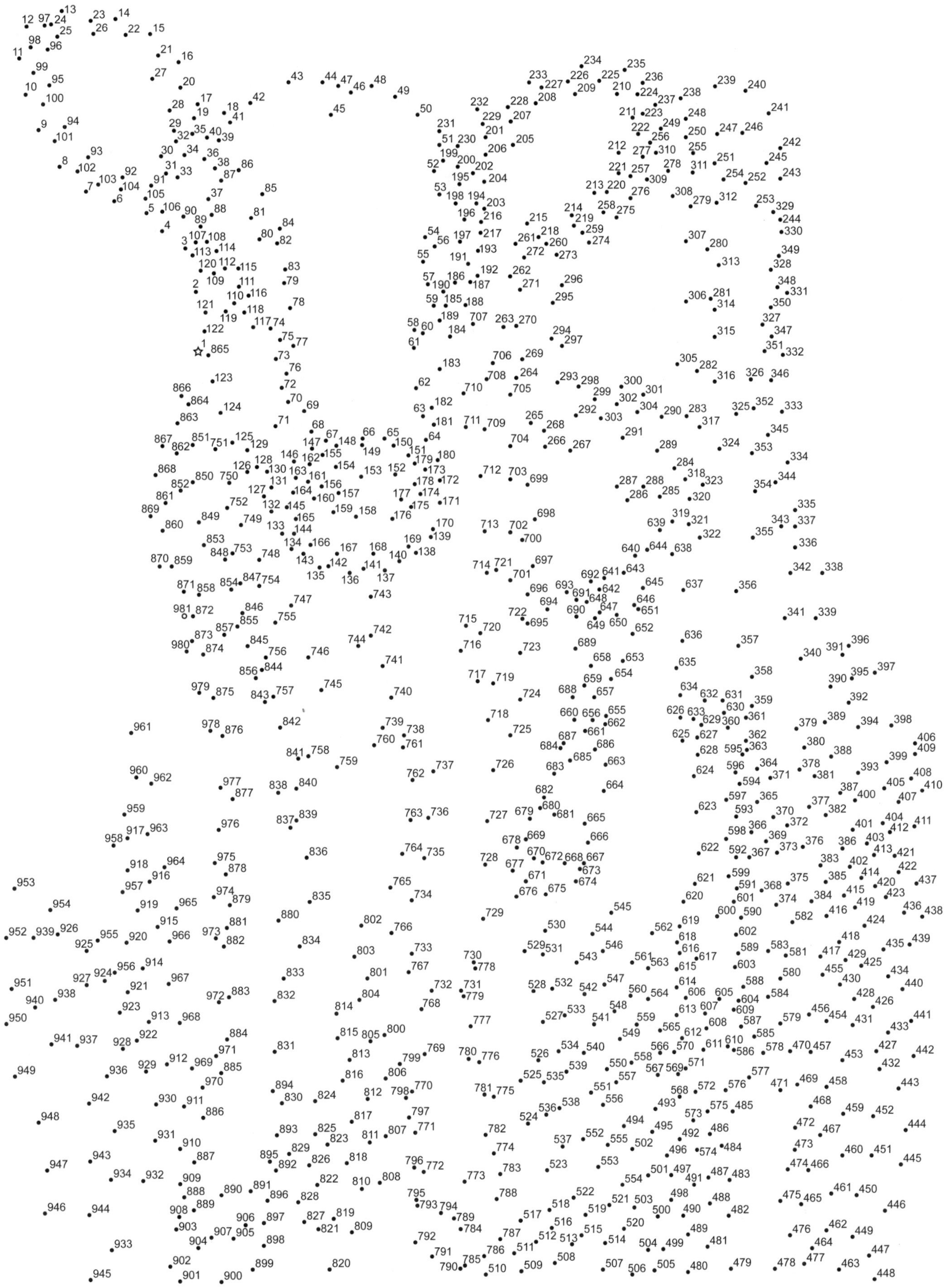

> Be kind to one another, tenderhearted, forgiving
> one another, as God in Christ forgave you.
>
> Ephesians 4:32 ESV

Sooner or later you'll run into someone who gets on your last nerve and stomps on it twice. Yet time and time again throughout the Bible you're reminded that whenever you run into relational conflict, you're called to love deep and hard and to forgive often.

It's tempting to think that harboring hostility toward someone only affects two people—you and the other person. But strife always spills into the lives of others. Why? Because hurt people hurt people.

Perhaps that's why forgiveness is a cornerstone characteristic of following Christ. To overcome a feud, we must forgive again and again and again. We must carry ourselves with a disposition of love—especially toward those for whom we feel it the least.

In which relationship in your life do you most need to repent and pursue a disposition of love?

READ • REFLECT • CONNECT • PRAY • JOURNAL

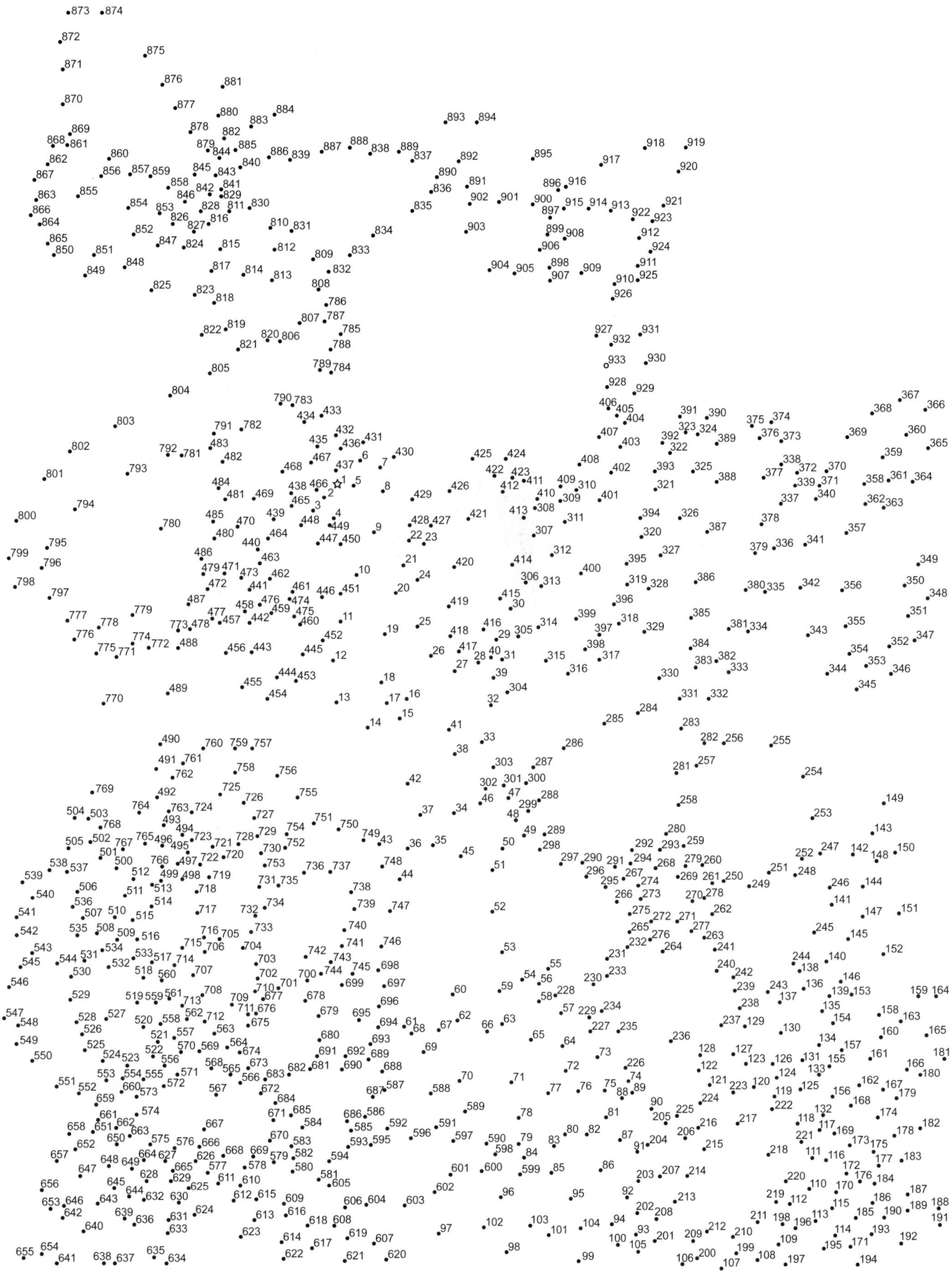

> Consider the lilies of the field, how they grow:
> they neither toil nor spin;
> and yet I say to you that even Solomon
> in all his glory was not arrayed like one of these.
>
> Matthew 6:28–29 NKJV

King Solomon is one of the greatest kings of Israel. As the son of King David, he becomes familiar with royal life as a youth. In 1 Kings 3, God asks Solomon what he would like from Him. Solomon's answer: wisdom. God is pleased with Solomon's response and gives him more power, wealth, and wisdom than any king before him. Solomon lives a privileged life of excess and grandeur.

Yet Jesus pauses to make a comparison between this mighty king and the everyday flowers that likely surrounded his palace. Solomon could afford the most exquisite clothing on the planet. Everyday flowers are incapable of making their own clothes or fashioning their own appearance, yet God dresses them in impeccable beauty. If God cares so tenderly for a flower that blossoms one day and withers the next, how much more does God care for us?

Recall three ways in which God has shown His tender care and lavish love for you.

READ • REFLECT • CONNECT • PRAY • JOURNAL

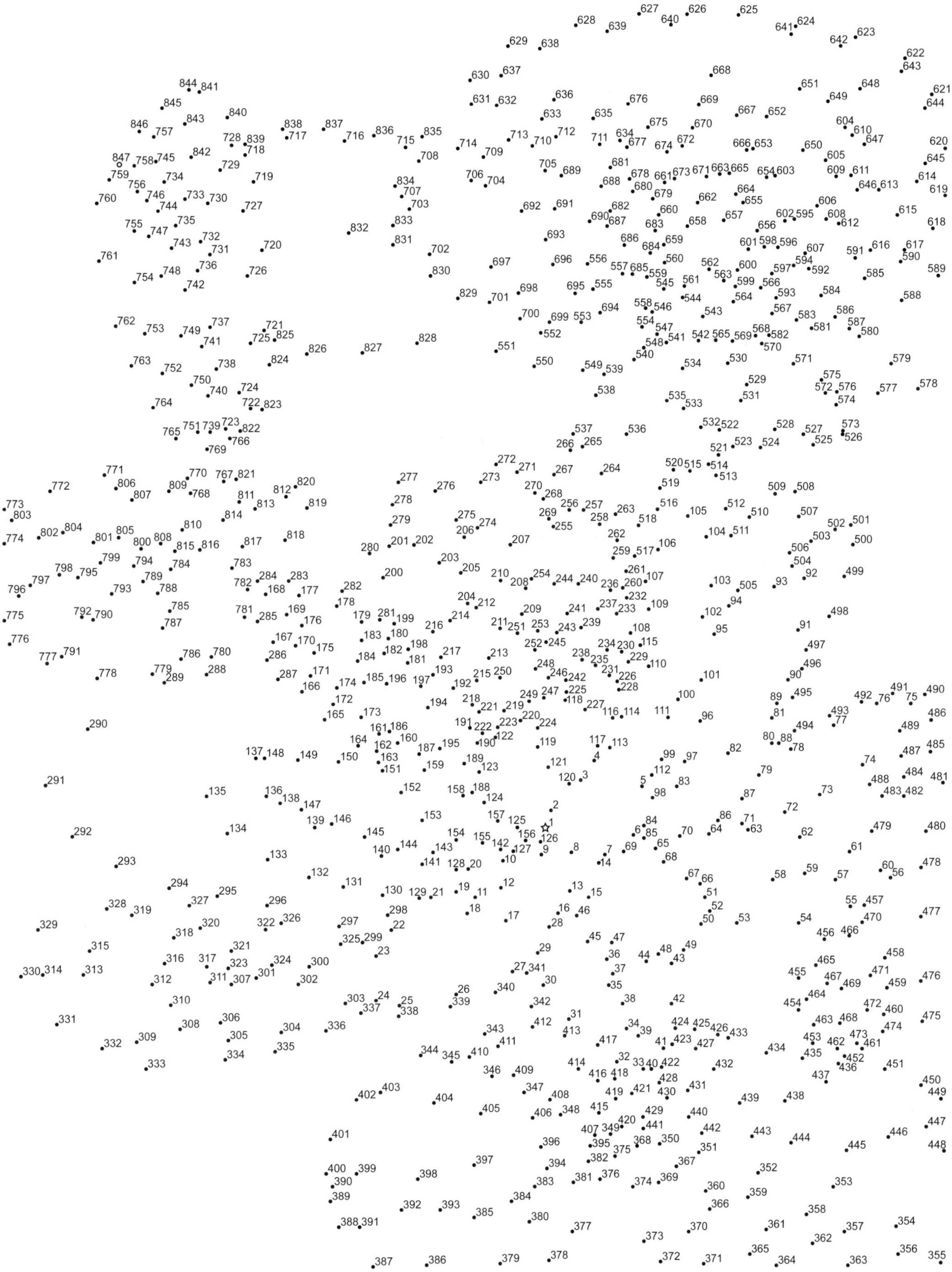

> And the Word was made flesh, and dwelt among us.
>
> John 1:14 KJV

When the children of Israel leave Egypt, God instructs them to build a tabernacle. This tent structure is shaped like a rectangle. The wooden frame is draped with curtains made of purple, indigo, and scarlet fabric symbolizing royalty and sacrifice. An inner room known as the holy of holies contains the ark of the covenant. Inside the ark rest the Ten Commandments, a gold container with manna, and Aaron's rod. The structure is constructed of the gold, silver, jewels, fabrics, and other precious materials the Israelites take when they leave Egypt.

The tabernacle serves as the sacred place for God to meet His people. The people gather there for worship and sacrifice. This is a portable meeting place for the Israelites to encounter God.

When Jesus arrives, He provides the perfect tabernacle. John 1:14 can be translated, "He became flesh and tabernacled among us." Jesus becomes our spiritual tabernacle where He serves as the High Priest. Through Him we have access to the presence of God.

Reflect on Jesus as the Immanuel, God with us. How have you experienced the presence of Christ in your life?

READ • REFLECT • CONNECT • PRAY • JOURNAL

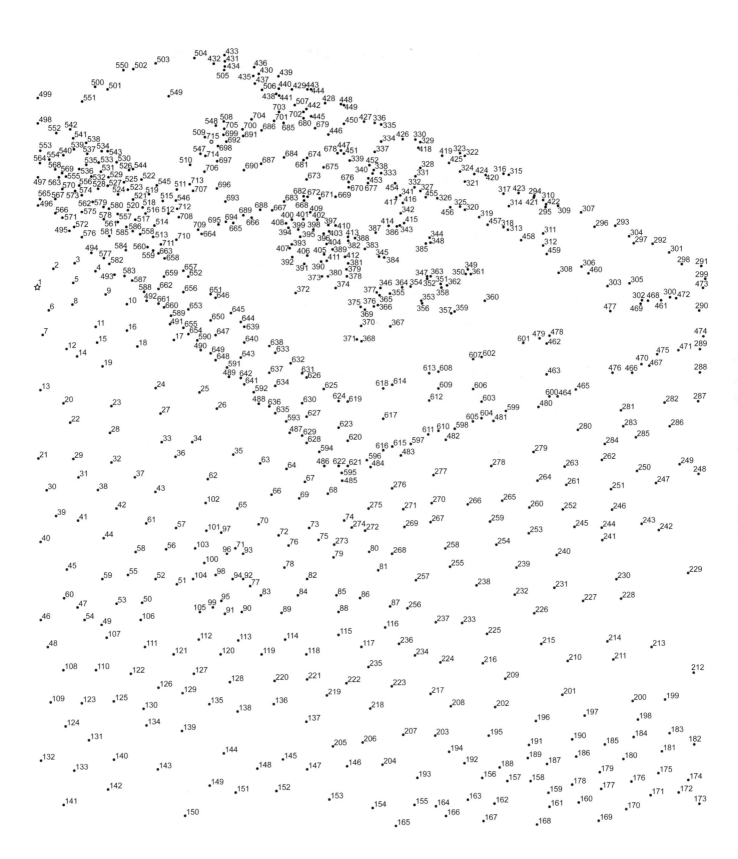

> Now faith is the substance of things hoped for,
> the evidence of things not seen.
>
> Hebrews 11:1 KJV

"Have faith." This well-meaning phrase is often issued like a Band-Aid to people facing difficult times. But what does it mean to have faith when the situation feels hopeless? What does it mean to have faith during loss or separation or sickness? When there is too much pain, too much affliction, too much loss?

Faith is the ability to recognize that what we see doesn't have the last word. Faith challenges us to remember that it's always darkest before the dawn. That we can overcome dark situations because Christ has overcome the darkest situation. He conquered the grave to bring us new life.

When you begin to doubt, stir up your faith by remembering the promises of God. Read through the Scriptures in this book and pay special attention to God's presence, faithfulness, provision, and goodness. Ground yourself in the truth of the character of God.

Write down three ways in which God has carried you through difficult times in the past. How does this strengthen your faith for what God will do in the future?

READ • REFLECT • CONNECT • PRAY • JOURNAL

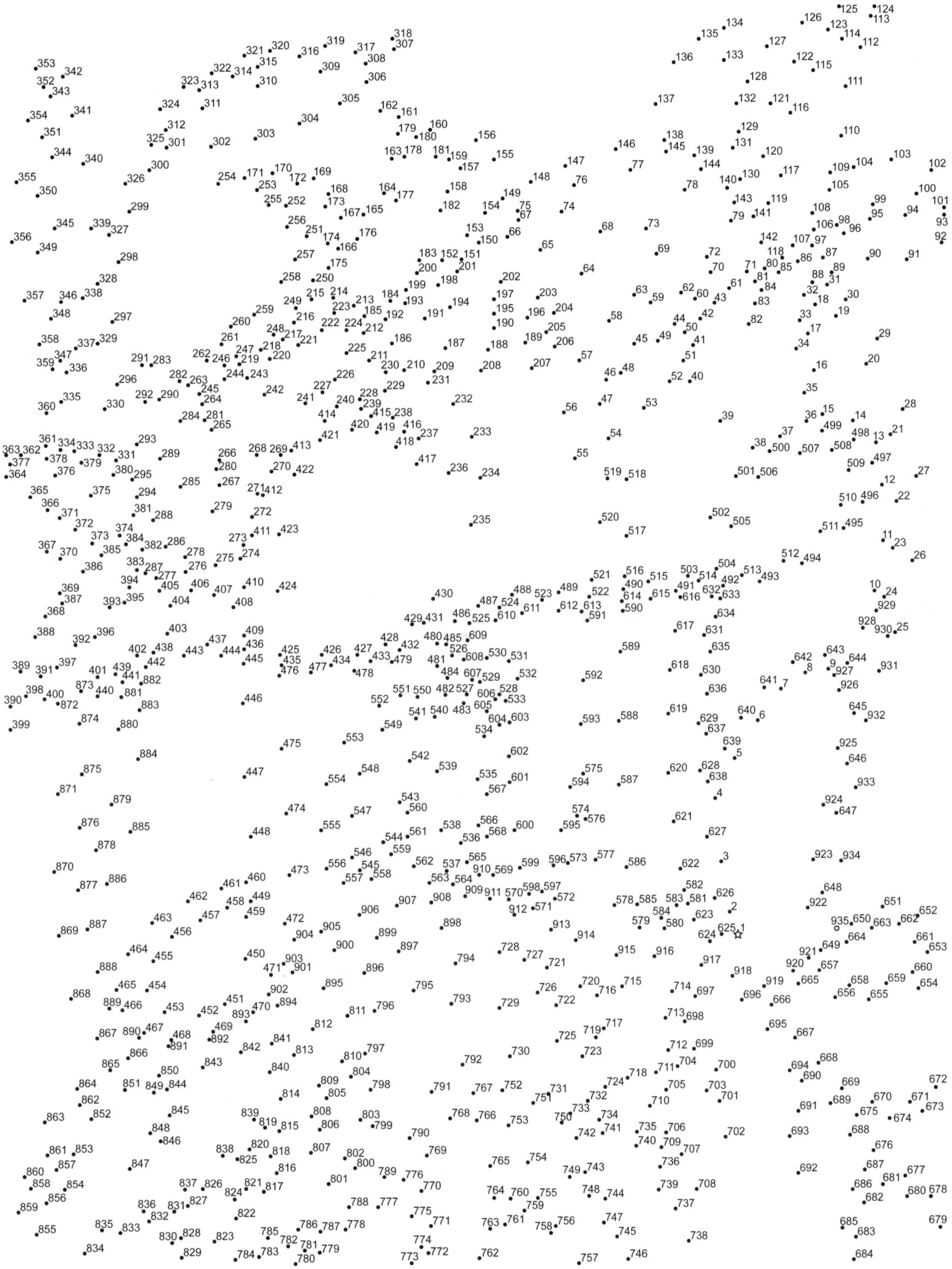

> But they who wait for the Lord shall renew their strength;
>
> they shall mount up with wings like eagles;
>
> they shall run and not be weary;
>
> they shall walk and not faint.
>
> Isaiah 40:31 ESV

Did you know that an eagle's grip is ten times stronger and its eyes are six times sharper than that of humans? These majestic birds of prey fly at speeds of thirty miles per hour and can dive at speeds of one hundred miles per hour.

In ancient Rome, eagles served as a symbol of power and strength. They still do today, especially as the United States' national bird.

The psalmist compares the strength of eagles to that of those who wait on the Lord. If we try to soar or succeed on our own, we soon grow tired and weary. Whenever we depend on ourselves, we fizzle out. But when we place our trust in God, we discover Him as the source of our renewal and strength. As we wait on God, we learn that He is faithful to infuse us with vigor and vitality we do not have on our own.

What situation is causing you the most exhaustion right now? Spend ten minutes in prayer asking God to renew your strength.

READ • REFLECT • CONNECT • PRAY • JOURNAL

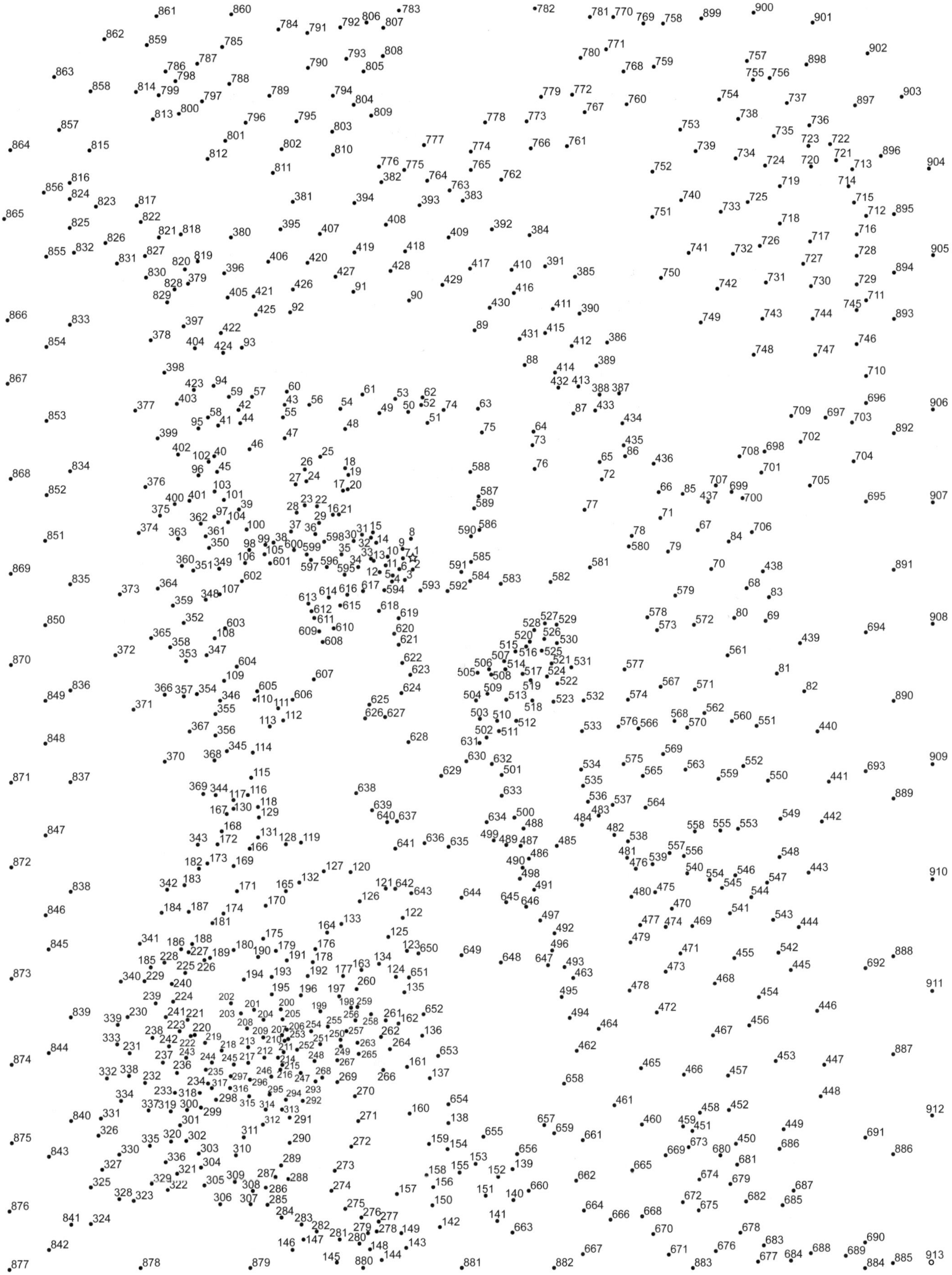

> The Lord's unfailing love and mercy still continue,
> fresh as the morning, as sure as the sunrise.
>
> Lamentations 3:22–23 GNT

Think of the last time you saw a sunrise that took your breath away. Splashes of crimson and streaks of fuchsia. Dots of burnt orange and dabs of canary yellow.

When the sun peeps over the horizon, light stretches through the atmosphere. Blues and purples dissipate and vibrant warm colors dart across the sky. As the sun rises higher throughout the day, the shorter wavelengths scatter, casting blues and purples once again.

The Master Artist paints a canvas each day for His glory and our delight. Even when life is shaky and uncertain, there are two constants: the morning sunrise and evening sunset. God wows us with His creativity and stuns us with His beauty. This rhythm of the skies reminds us of God's loving-kindness and faithful promises.

Set your alarm early enough to watch the sunrise one morning this week. Spend time drinking in the wonder and beauty of creation. Soak in the simple reminder of God's love and mercy available to you each and every day.

READ • REFLECT • CONNECT • PRAY • JOURNAL

> Deep calls to deep in the roar of your waterfalls;
> all your waves and breakers have swept over me.
>
> Psalm 42:7 NIV

Have you ever stood on the banks of a waterfall? Or crawled over the craggy rocks?

The psalmist describes the sound of water crashing from above, that moment your senses are dulled by all that's happening before you. All you can hear is the roar.

Sometimes that happens in life. All we can hear is the roar of the heartache or loss or pain. Yet the psalmist reminds us that even in those times, deep still cries to deep. You may feel swept away by the waters of fear, washed out by hardship, or overwhelmed by circumstances, but you are never alone. God remains with you. And God's voice is louder than the noise you're hearing. God's power is mightier than the adversity you're facing. God's love is stronger than the pain you're feeling.

In what area of your life do you most need to hear God's voice and experience God's presence?

READ • REFLECT • CONNECT • PRAY • JOURNAL

....

....

....

....

....

....

....

....

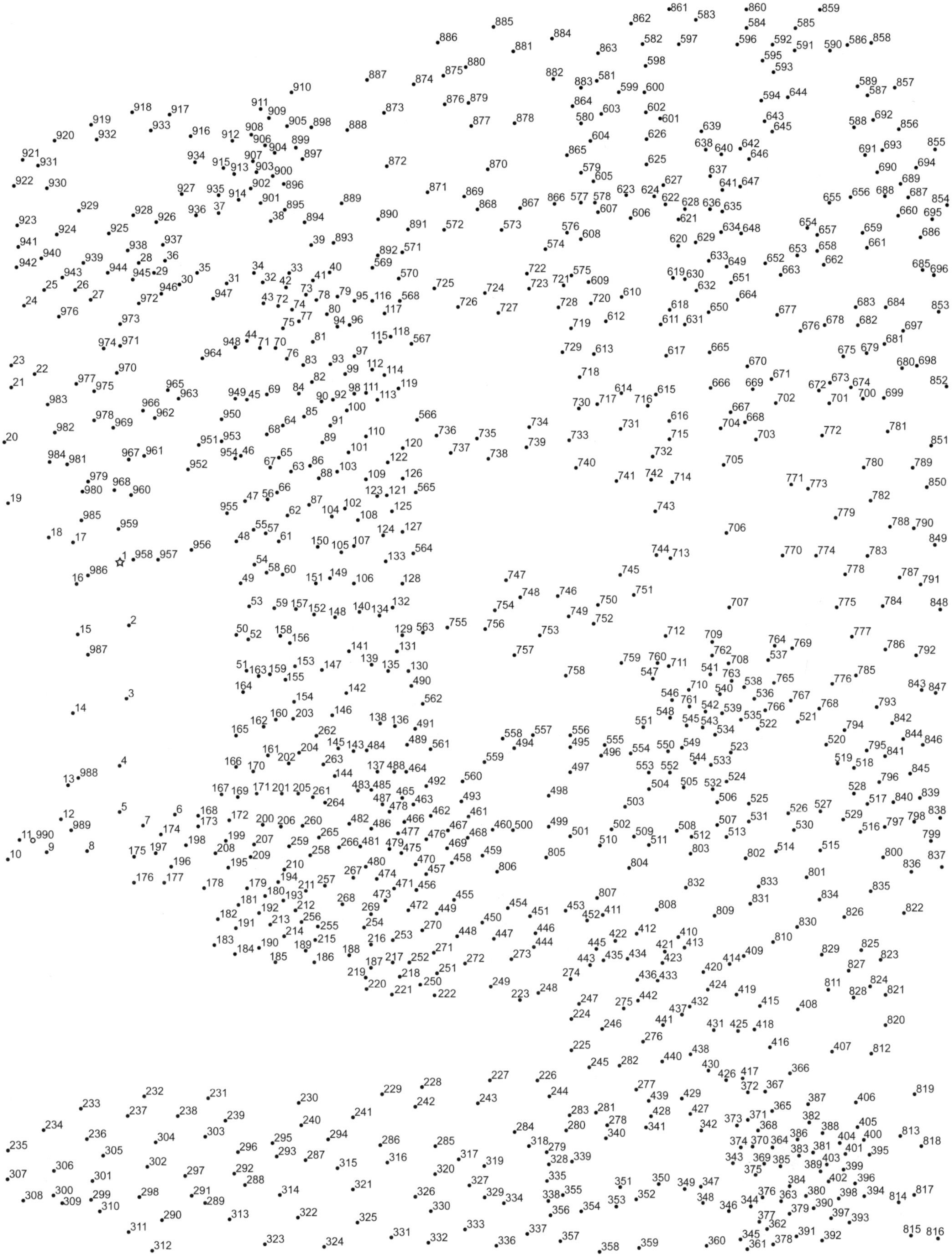

Meet Margaret

A self-described "hot mess," Margaret Feinberg is a popular Bible teacher and speaker at churches and leading conferences such as Catalyst, Thrive, and Women of Joy. Her books, including *The Organic God, The Sacred Echo, Scouting the Divine, Wonderstruck,* and *Fight Back With Joy* and their corresponding Bible studies, have sold more than one million copies and received critical acclaim and extensive national media coverage from CNN, the Associated Press, *USA Today,* the *Los Angeles Times,* the *Washington Post,* and more.

She was recently named one of 50 women most shaping culture and the church today by *Christianity Today,* one of the 30 voices who will help lead the church in the next decade by *Charisma Magazine,* and one of the 40 who will shape Christian publishing by *Christian Retailing* magazine. Margaret and her husband, Leif, have an adorable superpup named Hershey. She believes some of the best days are spent in jammies, laughing, and being silly.

Let's be friends

 margaretfeinberg.com

 Margaret Feinberg

 @mafeinberg

 @mafeinberg

 hello@margaretfeinberg.com

Lovelies Just for You

Fight Back With Joy

Through vulnerable storytelling, a difficult diagnosis, and a good dose of humor, Fight Back With Joy reveals how joy is more than whimsy. It's the weapon you can use to fight life's battles.

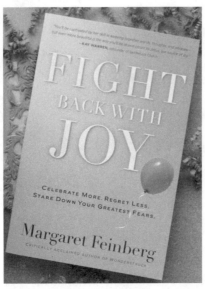

What to Say When You Don't Know What to Say Greeting Cards

These modern, bright n' beautiful cards are made to encourage and inspire. All are designed to equip you to help those facing tough times fight back with joy.

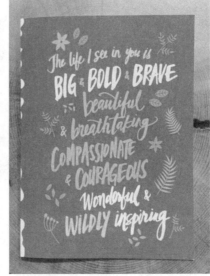

Flourish: 52-Week Devotional

Flourish offers a year of weekly devotions that will awaken your soul to a life of fullness and joy that spills over to bless others.

Fight Back With Joy: 6-Session DVD Bible Study

Dive deep into the Scripture in order to expand your joy threshold, beat back discouragement, and awaken God's fierce love for you. You'll be equipped with more than two dozen tactics to begin to fight back with joy no matter what battleground you're on.

Visit margaretfeinberg.com to find
fresh Bible studies, When You Don't Know What to Say cards,
and Scripture-based coloring books.